all the things my mother never told me

all the things my mother never told me

daniella deutsch

artwork by lisa jean moran

*atmosphere press*

a letter to my reader -

I am 25 years old. I know next to nothing. Although I do know one small thing - that the more years that pass, the more questions without answers begin to pile up. My primary response to this realization was panic, eventually followed by relief. And soon after, freedom. However, the transition from panic to freedom was far from smooth. And it took me almost a year and a half writing this book to come to experience that freedom. Being in my 20s is complex, as I am undoubtedly sure it is or was for you. The pain is ugly and the shock of it can be numbing. The bliss is just as loud as it is quiet and can even be addicting. I have come to comprehend that life is just as exhilarating as it is monotonous. The past few years have been my first true understanding of the human condition and what it means to be alive - to live with the knowledge that we can plan very little, therefore we can depend on nothing but change.

Grasping this idea hits hard. The 20s are dirty, euphoric, exhausting, jumbled, romantic, conflicting, and open ended. To be in our 20s means we spend our days cradling our deeply fragile goals, plans, dreams, relationships, finances, romances, and existential crises. And that's just on a Tuesday. Nothing is permanent. We live in limbo as our norm; yet no one prepares us for it. No one blatantly tells us that every decision we make will likely take an unexpected turn. No one warns you that your first love will not be your last. No one reminds us that our childhood dreams will disintegrate - but that we will dream new ones and be alright with that. No one tells us the fastest way to sober up, any tricks to get out of bed in the morning when we don't think we can, how to fall asleep at night after we've lost a job, or simply even how to do our taxes.

While living inside this decade, not even our mother's unconditional love shields us from defeat. But as the poet Wendell Berry writes, "The mind that is not baffled is not employed." His words comforted and inspired me. So, I sit, and I write. I tackle the decade, which I am only halfway through, by sharing unanswerable questions. By embracing them. By reaching out and holding the hands of every other person, just as shell shocked and unprepared to fight life's questions with no plausible answers.

I hope my collection of poems brings a sliver of peace to those who need it and makes the inevitable discomfort of being in our 20s feel somewhat comforting, because we are all just as lost as the next. These poems certainly do not encompass every single aspect of the 20s, but I have locked down many of the emotions I feel we must be more transparent about. We are all young and sweaty and tearful and tired, yet with much more to go. Our lives may look drastically different, but our emotions ring out similarly. These days and months and years are unexpected, lonely, magical, chaotic, unsettling, and sobering. There may not be many answers, but I believe that is enough of an answer in itself. The more we openly share the truth about the chaos, the easier it will be to make our way out of this decade sturdy on our two feet.

Please pass it on,

Daniella

*for my mother, who still told me more
than I could have ever dreamt up.*

# table of contents

on reality

I day dream
night dream
pulse
claw
scratch
for a dirty super 8 film life
a grainy fantasy covered in the good kind of blood
with blind eyes
I imagine premature bodies seething with coke
or perhaps it is actually only coffee
in former years I would have killed for
died for
lost myself for
an ultimate flood of angst
the beautifully fucked up and over cracked style of a day
so when I opened my eyes
after a comatose self fulfilled prophecy
I tell you now
if you itch for the cinematic crumble
as badly as I did
it will sure as hell happen
and it will not look glossed over
or orgasmic like you believe
it will burn up your insides
in ways that cannot be regrown
and then leave you
wrongly thinking there is an afterlife.

## I. on 23

I woke with a crashing
diving into new spaces and soot
far off from a thirsty land
but ready to sit steady for the oasis

## 2. on faith

this year held me in its palm like no other
gentle
yet demanding
braiding courage through my unloved thighs

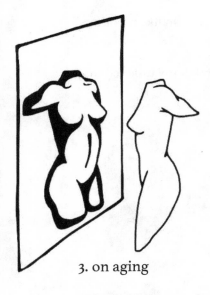

### 3. on aging

nobody likes you when you're 23
childhood rots from the inside out
adulthood snakes its way
down
down
down
you again
inhabiting your soul with sweet dedication
cradling parts of your body which frankly you despise
all you hear at night
is the achy dishwasher lull
and your therapist's words echoing in your sleep

## 4. on the five years

in these last moments
I feel I know you better this summer in my mind
than I ever did with your shape right in front of me
diving into hindsight
I now love you more through memories
than my dry fingers believed I could
when I first sat down
to pour myself a glass of me

## 5. on panicking

I wake up
everywhere itches
vibrations of the world have stuck to me
I grow sick of the gift of healing
so now
I wake up
I peel them off
expose the dark crusty scabs
to the air conditioned bedroom
wince with delight
taste my own blood
say sorry to my pain
and go back to sleep
to claw myself through another REM cycle

## 6. on saviors

I would be lifeless
on the corner of Broadway and 22nd
if it were not for selfless ink
a seeping wet invitation
and the slate from the crumbling trees
for writers have a cure
sweet bitter medicine to save their souls
to bind the chaos safely together
while the rest of the world winks and fails them

## 7. on numbness

perhaps my mind is for sale now
half off
and in decent condition
it is 80 degrees
I almost forgot
I will be fed a slice of anniversary tonight
the champagne bottle shell is at the bottom
of a swimming pool filled with indifference
what I mean to say is
this is the most boring mouthful of pain
I swear it over and over
riding the subway I stand myself backwards
for some type of a thrill
a single boulevard once had me crawling and
now 'I've been through worse'
is a dangerous game—
I may let the champagne drown me

## 8. on self-care

I grow out my hair to expose my many secrets
I bite off my nails to dispose of any charm
forgive me if I appear more daring now
less polite to strangers
and far more to myself

## 9. on inertia

my saliva is mostly salt today
piling up in my combative throat
a cotton mouth from cursing—
have I not been here before? I ask the man who sits
like a Buddha in my subway station
his dog blinks to the beat of my worn down heart
I spent last night in an emotional coma of flavors
I tell them
tastes I thought I had spit out
webs of words
bubbling only when night waves hello
now I am spinning from needles
eating out my mind for breakfast
are these not the paths I already flooded over?
how many times
can I rip down flights of my own body's stairs?

## 10. on soulmates

how strangely sad
we meet more people in our timid time
than we will ever count
yet it is so very rare
to find one
who looks deep enough into your soul
to see their very own

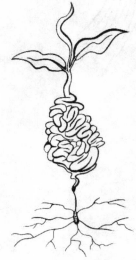

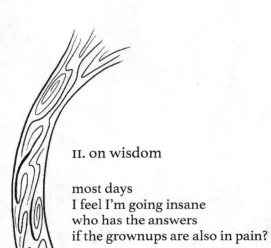

## ii. on wisdom

most days
I feel I'm going insane
who has the answers
if the grownups are also in pain?

## 12. on desperation

April is angry with me
I swear it
I curse it
please etch the answers
in my skin
spike my blood with
godly
knowledge
from a religion I do not believe in
slip my veins
the poison please
before I give up on this unearthly equation

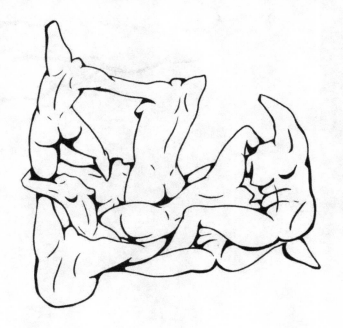

## 13. on letting go

the first snow always makes me think of you
I just came from the clouds
as well
crossed over the finish line—
doesn't it feel splendid to be complete?
you are still all over me inside the wet
but do not be fooled
I never write about the greats

## 14. on giving advice

did I go wrong
when I poured every centimeter of me into the rest of
them?
because I cannot seem to locate any more juice in my lungs
it has long since disappeared
disintegrated
I am depleted of the past's passion
go ask someone new to solve your puzzled woes
I am knee deep in my own brain
and you my friend, had your chance

15.  on sex

'so tell me about you'
he whispers
on a 20 degree night uptown
the tall buildings bite off my sanity
'fuck ton of feelings'
I smile
as he looks at the pillow and slides himself inside of me

## 16. on breaking promises

there is humor
in swearing never to return to a spiral
I melt easily
brainwashed
tracing an infinity maze
bleeding out my sanity
for one breath per night
haunted by
circles and
twisters
the promise to glue my feet in drying concrete
and declaration to never resort
tortures me
unraveling sensations tickle my logic
rendering precious vision inaccessible
tempting me in waves I swear I had outgrown
I can smell it
rattling my sacred bones
I peek back
petrified of the foreboding human mind
I fear I may crumble
curl
nod
to the face who willingly dips her toes back in
it is all so disgusting and I am in love with it
now I am afraid I truly would shake hell's hand
this morning I gasp—
am I here?

## 17. on denial

some days
strangers on the subway
look at me for longer
than you did

## 18. on extroversion

outward bound: the language of my spirit my whole life
toppling forward into
words
skin
breath
and bones
pieces of you and you and you glowing up my insides
a layman's super power rocking
between graceful and turbulent waves
connected to pulsating characters
looking deep enough I saw seeping glittery gore
between cracks of unfinished smiles
and detected detached desires underneath steely bodies
yet now I feel my planet's heartbeat is fainter
and I wonder if you dug it out of me
kidnapped
and
executed
these molecules of matter in a different time zone
or if perhaps I gave it away
and brainwashed myself into believing you would nurture it

### 19. on progress

someone told me
it would take a lot of time
I do not know who told me
but I think the voice may have been mine

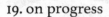

## 20. on playing with fire

you
yes you, took a lighter
from your pocket
lit the wick of my body
into a prancing flame
felt the heat warm your fingertips
put the lighter back in your pocket
and blew out the candle

## 21. on karma

put your trust in the universe
an admirable psychic says
I'll put out my hands
and lay down my heart
although my trust is another tale
my trust is now for sale
and it comes at a heavy price

## 22. on vices

I set fear in the corner
on an unwarranted time out
I'd rather the truth boring and clean
than a lie saddled up in a bow
sadness is easier sipping smoke up to my knees
and being stuck underground
is the freest I have felt
since I scraped myself together
to make this city a home

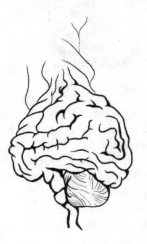

## 23. on infatuation

your own skin alone
writes my greatest works of poetry
but where will it all go
the day the page is not enough?

### 24. on truth

girls are always women
because we have to be
from the start
men are always boys
because the world allows them to be
and they do not object

## 25. on new homes

just like that
my hometown grabs another dreamer
sucking them in
to the smoggy tunnel I escaped as soon as I could bolt
my legs snap into the only split I can manage
reaching to coax the bodies back
each horn more deafening than the last
as 9pm turns to 6pm
my jealous blood curls
unjust
and
ravenous
I hear my name scattered with dirty thirst
I swear my heart has skymiles

**26. on a party I was not invited to**

all my heartbreaks dine together
feasting over cherries and pomegranates and sausage and wine
one broke in a minute
another took eight months
one broke with slick intention
another with murky shock
one broke with hellish allegiance
the other with salty fear
one broke with inertia for half a decade long
another cracked simply in one foggy day
all my heartbreaks dine together
I must have misplaced the invitation

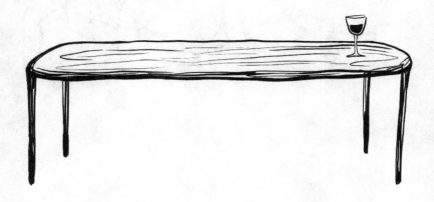

## 27. on forgiveness

I found
you must be strong
in order to be weak
once you collapse your own self down
like an eggshell deck of playing cards
you then have permission
to rise up higher
than your weakest body
ever imagined for your most triumphant mind

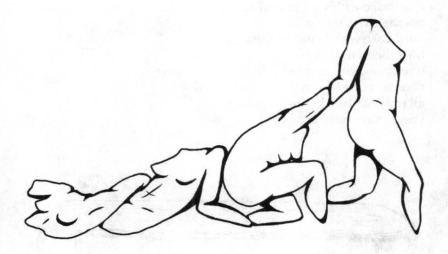

## 28. on commitment

it is foolish to believe
that stripping down
seals any deal
it is childish to believe
that exchanging moans
promises a sliver of allegiance
it is wrong to believe
that hands on a face
and underneath
and behind
and on top
mean you will not simply
disappear
into air
and be
there
and then
be
not

## 29. on survival

New York, baby
I wrote to you today
a love letter through telepathy
inching nice and close to the bridge's fingers
I lick the rusty dust from underneath my nail
peer over to ignite the scratchy calls
and proudly back my worthy outline away
peeling off each aftershock with a sideways grin
for now I believe I am finding myself
even as if it is through gravel
slow yet tough
tough like my grandfather's fresco worn hands
like my sister's bones which refuse to crack
I inhale through
reincarnated
lungs
attaching my emptied body
to a city filled to the brim

## on exhaling

here is where we tear out the truth
I admit the dirt is the single soul I trust
I watch as we all go to war
with ourselves
again
for time inside my own skin passes slowly
this year
tell me, is it not the same for you?
yet I have come to climb the walls of my brain each day
with more speed
peering over my uneven shoulders last night
I like what I see
it is a glorious sight
to pack up
and roll one's self back into her body again
so we applaud
and mimic each other proudly
with careful compassion
chins high
dripping with melancholic admiration
and the soft understanding that this is only the beginning
a gentle moment to blink inside breath is rare
so I choose to share my sweet solitude with you all,
that I can promise
just this morning a strong inhale filled my lungs
with my mother's very own blood
for one single moment
I let go
and that is a gift.

## acknowledgments

Everyone who helped get me here, you know who you are. But just as a reminder: thank you to those who sat with me late into the night or early in the morning reviewing every single line. Thank you to the small nooks and crannies in Brooklyn & Manhattan for being the battlegrounds in which I poured my heart out - especially Hungry Ghost Coffee on Metropolitan Avenue. Thank you to all the moments and humans who held my hand and filled the first half of this decade with more than enough strength to power through this process with hope. Thank you to those who broke my heart, giving me more to write about. Thank you to the many members of my family for gladly reading more drafts than they ever asked for and for showing me unconditional support and enthusiasm. Thank you to my hero of a therapist for offering me her hand as I jump into the unknown, over and over. Thank you to SZA for writing the song '20 Something,' one of my greatest inspirations. Thank you to Atmosphere for taking a chance on me. Lastly, thank you to Lisa for welcoming this passion project with an open heart and for giving me the art of my dreams and a friendship for a lifetime.

## about atmosphere press

Atmosphere Press is an independent, full-service publisher for excellent books in all genres and for all audiences. Learn more about what we do at atmospherepress.com.

We encourage you to check out some of Atmosphere's latest releases, which are available at Amazon.com and via order from your local bookstore:

*Big Man Small Europe*, poetry by Tristan Niskanen
*In the Cloakroom of Proper Musings,* a lyric narrative by Kristina Moriconi
*Lucid_Malware.zip,* poetry by Dylan Sonderman
*The Unordering of Days*, poetry by Jessica Palmer
*It's Not About You,* poetry by Daniel Casey
*A Dream of Wide Water,* poetry by Sharon Whitehill
*Radical Dances of the Ferocious Kind*, poetry by Tina Tru
*The Woods Hold Us,* poetry by Makani Speier-Brito
*My Cemetery Friends: A Garden of Encounters at Mount Saint Mary in Queens, New York,* nonfiction and poetry by Vincent J. Tomeo
*Report from the Sea of Moisture,* poetry by Stuart Jay Silverman
*The Enemy of Everything,* poetry by Michael Jones
*The Stargazers,* poetry by James McKee
*The Pretend Life,* poetry by Michelle Brooks
*Minnesota and Other Poems,* poetry by Daniel N. Nelson
*Interviews from the Last Days,* sci-fi poetry by Christina Loraine

Daniella Deutsch is a 25-year-old originally from Los Angeles, California. She migrated to New York as soon as she could, attending Skidmore College and is currently at NYU for a Masters in Clinical Social Work. Daniella has had pieces published by online literary journals such as *Ink and Voices*, *Little Death Lit*, and *5x5 Literary Magazine*. Her print publications include *In Parentheses Literary Magazine*, and another piece of hers is set to run in this winter's issue of *Gargoyle Magazine*. Daniella is a lover of city rooftops, fresh pasta, packed concert venues, and the feeling of buying far too many new books on a whim.

Lisa Jean Moran grew up in the woods of Ridgefield, Connecticut where her connection with nature was born. She now lives and works in New York City, teaching middle school Math, writing and performing original music, and spending time with her pet turtle Ronnie. Lisa has also recently produced a tarot deck, "Flow Tarot," fully written and illustrated by herself.

CPSIA information can be obtained
at www.ICGtesting.com
Printed in the USA
BVHW031610241120
594111BV00001B/41